JAN 2 7 2010

D1312442

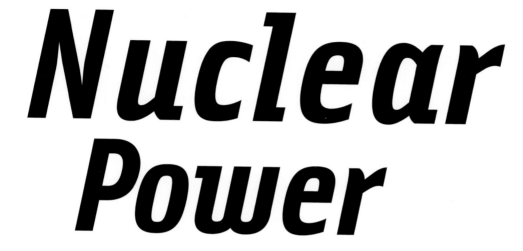

Nuclear Power

Chris Oxlade

A+

Smart Apple Media

Smart Apple Media
P.O. Box 3263, Mankato, Minnesota 56002

Printed in the United States

Published by arrangement with the Watts Publishing Group Ltd, London.

Library of Congress Cataloging-in-Publication Data

Oxlade, Chris.
  Nuclear power / Chris Oxlade.
      p. cm. -- (Science in the news)
  Includes index.
  ISBN 978-1-59920-320-1 (hardcover)
  1. Nuclear energy--Juvenile literature. 2. Nuclear facilities--Juvenile literature. 3. Nuclear engineering--Juvenile literature. I. Title.
  TK9148.O95 2010
  621.48'3--dc22

                                     2008049277

Design: Billin Design Solutions
Editor in Chief: John C. Miles
Editor: Sarah Ridley
Art Director: Jonathan Hair
Picture research: Diana Morris
Artwork: John Alston pages 18/19; Jason Billin map page 29

Picture credits
AKG Images: 10 inset. Albanpix/Rex Features: 34. Dimitri Beliakov/Rex Features: 21bl. Bettmann/Corbis: 27. Bildarchiv Pisarek/AKG Images: 10 main. Martin Bond/SPL: front cover, 1, 25, 48. Charles O. Cecil/Image Works/Topfoto: 14. Ecologie en Bretagne: 36. EFDA/JET/SPL: 2-3, 39bl. Gelpi/Shutterstock: 4. Tommaso Guicciardini/SPL: 40. Craig Hanson/Shutterstock: 13. Philippe Hays/Rex Features: 12. Edward Hirst /Rex Features: 31. Herbie Knott/Rex Features: 5b. Patrick Landmann/SPL: 41. Jerry Mason/SPL: 39tr. Greg Mathieson/Rex Features: 32. Petr Pavlicek/IAEA: 37. Photri/Topham: 15, 46-47. Picturepoint/Topfoto: 11. Kristina Postnikova/Shutterstock: 5c. Alan Pryke/Newspix/Rex Features: 16, 17cl. Phiiippe Psaila/SPL: 24. Chris Rainier/ Corbis: 20. RIA/Novosti/Topfoto: 17br, 22, 26, 28. Sipa Press/Rex Features: 23, 29, 30, 33. Ullstein Bild/Topfoto: 35. US Dept of Energy/SPL: 38. Watts: 21tr.

9 8 7 6 5 4 3 2 1

CONTENTS

WHAT IS NUCLEAR POWER?   8

THE HISTORY OF NUCLEAR POWER   10

WHO USES NUCLEAR POWER?   12

NUCLEAR FUELS   14

NUCLEAR POWER PLANTS   16

NUCLEAR REACTORS   18

NUCLEAR POWER FOR TRANSPORTATION   20

NUCLEAR WASTE   22

BUILDING AND DECOMMISSIONING   24

NUCLEAR SAFETY   26

THE CHERNOBYL DISASTER   28

TERROR THREATS   30

ROGUE STATES   32

ANTINUCLEAR PROTESTS   34

PLANS FOR NUCLEAR POWER   36

NUCLEAR FUSION   38

THE NUCLEAR FUTURE   40

GLOSSARY   42

WEB SITES   43

INDEX   44

WHAT IS NUCLEAR POWER?

NUCLEAR POWER is the use of nuclear energy to produce electricity. Nuclear energy is energy released during nuclear reactions, when atoms split apart or join together. Nuclear power is controversial because nuclear fuel is dangerously radioactive and linked to nuclear weapons.

WHY NUCLEAR POWER?

The main advantage of nuclear power is that, unlike fossil fuel power plants, nuclear power plants do not emit the greenhouse gas carbon dioxide. In fact, they release little pollution at all. Countries that have nuclear power plants are also less reliant on finding sources of fossil fuels (coal, oil, and gas), making them more "energy independent."

▲ A nuclear power plant. There is a reactor under each dome.

AND WHY NOT?

The main problem with nuclear power is the deadly radiation that comes from nuclear fuel waste. After it has been used, the fuel stays radioactive for thousands of years, so we are leaving a dangerous legacy for future generations. There is also a danger of accidents or terrorist attacks releasing radioactive materials from nuclear power plants.

HOW IT WORKS

The heart of a nuclear power plant is the nuclear reactor. Here, nuclear fuel takes part in nuclear reactions, which release heat energy. Just as in fossil fuel power plants, the heat is used to boil water to make steam, and the steam drives turbines that drive electric generators.

GET THE FACTS STRAIGHT

Nuclear reactions release a vast amount of energy.

- In a nuclear reaction, matter is turned to energy. About .036 ounces (1 g) of matter is equivalent to 100 million million joules—enough to run a light bulb for 150,000 years.

- Uranium nuclear fuel releases 20,000 times as much energy as burning the same amount of coal.

IN THE NEWS

Because of its controversial nature, nuclear power regularly makes the news headlines. Stories cover new developments in nuclear power technology, the opening of new plants, accidents that allow radiation to leak, or protests against nuclear power.

▼ A container of nuclear waste on a train. It displays the international radioactive warning symbol (inset).

THE HISTORY OF NUCLEAR POWER

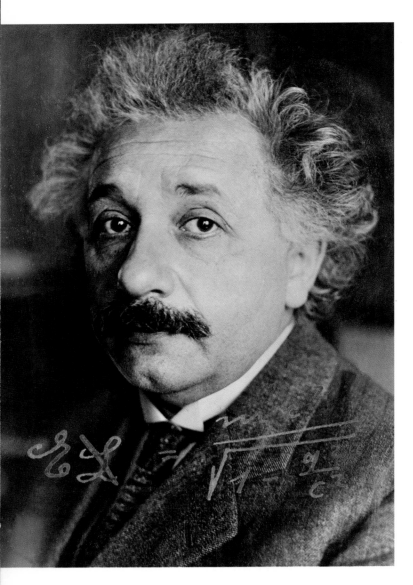

▲ Albert Einstein (1879–1955) was the first scientist to recognize the astonishing power of nuclear reactions.

THE FIRST STEP to nuclear power was made by the famous scientist Albert Einstein. In 1905, Einstein published his theory of special relativity. Contained in it was the famous equation $E=mc^2$, which shows that energy (E) and mass (m) are the same thing (c is the speed of light). In a nuclear reaction, mass is changed into energy.

FISSION DISCOVERED

In the late 1930s, a team of nuclear physicists in Berlin, including the Austrian Lise Meitner and the German Otto Hahn, were investigating the effect of bombarding atoms with neutrons. They discovered that some large atoms split in half, forming two smaller atoms, which they had thought was impossible. This nuclear reaction is now called nuclear fission.

THE FIRST REACTOR

Nuclear fission is caused when a neutron hits a large, unstable atom. When the atom splits, it releases more neutrons. Scientists realized that the fission of one atom would cause the fission of others around it, so that a chain reaction could be set up. The first experimental nuclear reactor began working in the United States in 1942.

NUCLEAR POWER BEGINS

The first nuclear reactor to produce electricity was EBR-I, in Idaho, which began operating in 1951. The U.S. government poured money into nuclear research, and in 1954, the head of the U.S. Atomic Energy Commission announced that nuclear power promised "electricity too cheap to meter." The first commercial nuclear power plant was at Calder Hall, Cumbria, in the United Kingdom, opened in 1956. Rapid development of nuclear power followed.

FACING THE ISSUES

The first reactors were built not for nuclear power but to produce plutonium, the fuel needed for nuclear weapons, which the United States was developing during World War II. After World War II, nuclear research continued in secret in many countries as they developed technology for both nuclear power and nuclear weapons.

▼ Queen Elizabeth II at the opening of the world's first commercial nuclear power plant at Calder Hall in the United Kingdom.

WHO USES NUCLEAR POWER?

A TOTAL OF 31 COUNTRIES

have nuclear power. There are more than 400 nuclear power plants in all, which provide about 6 percent of the world's electricity. Some countries use a high proportion of nuclear energy and some a low proportion. While some countries have been using nuclear power for decades, others plan never to use it.

IN THE UNITED STATES

The United States produces the largest amount of nuclear energy of any country—about 20 percent of all the electricity generated in the Untied States. The last new U.S. nuclear power plant opened in 1996. The United States also has nuclear-powered aircraft carriers and submarines.

EUROPEAN POWER

European countries have different policies on nuclear power. The United Kingdom now generates 20 percent of its electricity from nuclear power. France began its nuclear program in the 1970s, when oil prices soared. Spain, the Netherlands, Belgium, and several other European countries have nuclear power plants.

▲ The cooling tower of a French nuclear plant. France generates a massive 80 percent of its electricity from nuclear power.

▲ A nuclear power plant provides electricity for the port city of Lianynugang, China.

RUSSIA

The former Soviet Union developed nuclear reactors in the 1950s and had the first operational nuclear power plant in 1955. Russia now generates 16 percent of its electricity in nuclear power plants and is constructing nuclear power ships to supply electricity to cities on its remote northern coast. The Chernobyl accident (See pages 28–29) happened in the Soviet Union in 1986.

CHINA AND INDIA

China and India are undergoing rapid industrial growth and have a huge demand for electricity to power factories and the everyday needs of their large populations. Both use nuclear power as well as coal-fired power plants and are building new nuclear reactors. They are set to be two of the largest users of nuclear power, with plans to open more plants in the future.

GET THE FACTS STRAIGHT

- New Zealand and Ireland have decided never to use nuclear power.
- Italy shut down four nuclear power plants following a referendum held after the Chernobyl disaster in 1986.
- Germany is phasing out nuclear power.

NUCLEAR FUELS

THERE ARE ONLY TWO nuclear fuels used in power plants: uranium (U) and plutonium (Pu). The fuel is shaped into fuel rods that fit into a reactor. When the reactor is running, the atoms of these fuels split apart when they are hit by neutrons, thereby releasing energy.

URANIUM

Uranium is the only naturally-occurring chemical element that undergoes fission. On average it makes up just 0.0003 percent of the Earth's crust, but it is more abundant in some rocks than others. It is always found in combination with other elements. For example, in combination with oxygen (uranium dioxide), it is known as pitchblende. The main producers of uranium ore are Canada and Australia. There are also mines in Africa.

▼ A vast open-pit uranium ore mine in Niger, Africa.

► Nuclear fuel rods being prepared before their insertion into a reactor core.

ISOTOPES AND ENRICHMENT

All atoms are made up of three tiny particles —protons, neutrons, and electrons. The protons and neutrons are packed together in an atom's central nucleus. The nucleus of a uranium atom always has 92 protons. It can have either 146 neutrons, when it is called uranium-238 (U-238), or 143 neutrons, when it is called U-235. These different forms are called isotopes. Only U-235 undergoes fission. Natural uranium is about 99 percent U-238 and 1 percent U-235. To make fuel, the amount of U-235 is increased to about 4 percent. This process is called enrichment.

PLUTONIUM

Plutonium is produced artificially from uranium in nuclear reactors. It is made when uranium-238 absorbs a neutron given off by fission reactions in the reactor. The isotope of plutonium formed is Pu-239.

FACING THE ISSUES

One of the criticisms of nuclear power is that supplies of uranium are running out. The known reserves of high-grade uranium ore (that contains up to 2 percent uranium) will last only until the end of the twenty-first century. However, the nuclear industry insists that there are thousands of years' worth of uranium available in the form of low-grade ores, currently too expensive to mine.

NUCLEAR POWER PLANTS

IN A NUCLEAR POWER PLANT, the job of the nuclear reactor is to produce heat. The heat is carried away from the reactor by a coolant and then used to boil water to make steam. The steam rushes through turbines, making them spin, and the turbines spin generators that produce electricity.

▼ Workers examine the reinforced vessel that will contain a nuclear reactor at a new research facility in Australia.

A CHAIN REACTION

The nuclear reactions that produce heat happen inside the core of a nuclear reactor. There are dozens of fuel rods in the core. Atoms of fuel in the fuel elements split apart, releasing heat energy and neutrons. The neutrons hit other atoms of fuel, making them split, too. So a chain reaction is set up in the core that continues releasing heat.

IN CONTROL

Parts of the reactor called control rods control the speed of the chain reaction, which in turn controls the heat output from the reactor. The control rods are made of boron or cadmium, which absorb neutrons, stopping the neutrons from keeping the chain reaction going. When the control rods are fully inserted into the reactor core, the chain reaction stops. The farther they are retracted, the faster the chain reaction goes, the more heat is released, and the more electricity is generated. Control rods are part of the safety system of the reactor, as inserting them completely shuts the reactor down.

◀ Inside a reactor research center. Nuclear fuel is extremely radioactive and must be handled with great care (See below).

FACING THE ISSUES

The radiation from nuclear fuel and other materials used in the nuclear industry is extremely harmful. Large doses of radiation in a short time damage vital organs and cause a condition called radiation sickness, which often kills the victim within a few days or weeks. Exposure to low doses of radiation over a long time can cause cancers. Workers in nuclear power plants wear special equipment that records their exposure to radiation.

▲ A radiation exposure badge (or dosimeter) records its wearer's exposure to radiation.

NUCLEAR REACTORS

THERE ARE SEVERAL different types of nuclear reactor. Each has a different core design and a different cooling system. However, most are in a family of reactors called thermal reactors. The others are called breeder reactors.

THERMAL REACTORS

In a thermal reactor, each fuel rod is surrounded by a material called a moderator. The moderator's job is to slow down the fast neutrons released by the splitting atoms of fuel. The neutrons need to be slowed because slow neutrons have a much better chance of causing fission in other atoms. Common moderators are graphite and "heavy" water (water that contains deuterium—a type of hydrogen).

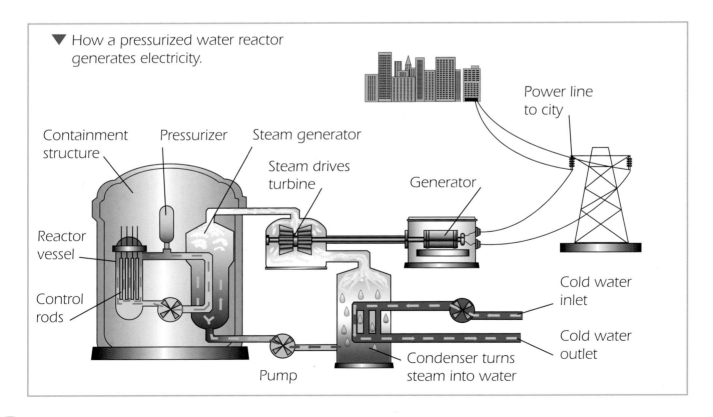

▼ How a pressurized water reactor generates electricity.

Power line to city

Containment structure

Pressurizer

Steam generator

Steam drives turbine

Generator

Reactor vessel

Control rods

Cold water inlet

Cold water outlet

Pump

Condenser turns steam into water

THERMAL REACTOR TYPES

Two common types of thermal reactor are the pressurized water reactor (PWR) and the advanced gas-cooled reactor (AGR). In the pressurized water reactor, the water (which can be heavy water or ordinary "light" water) is both the moderator, slowing the neutrons, and the coolant, carrying heat away from the reactor. In the advanced gas-cooled reactor, the moderator is graphite, and the coolant is carbon dioxide gas.

FAST BREEDER REACTORS

There is no moderator to slow the neutrons in a fast breeder reactor, so the neutrons are all "fast." To make up for this, breeder reactors use highly enriched fuel so that the fast neutrons can keep the reaction going.

Around the reactor core is a blanket of uranium. When fast neutrons hit this, some of the uranium-238 atoms are turned into plutonium, which can then be used as a fuel in the reactor. So the reactor "breeds" fuel.

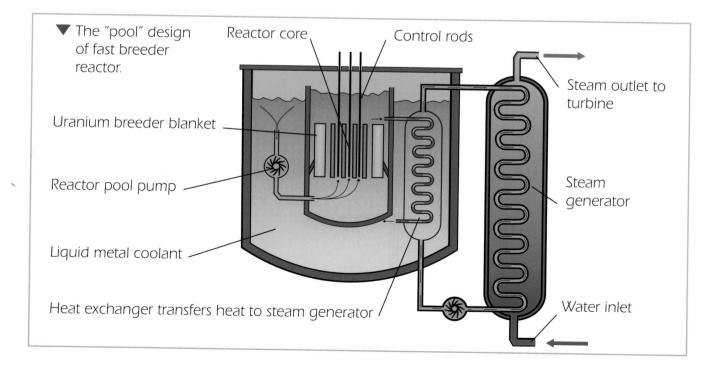

▼ The "pool" design of fast breeder reactor.

Reactor core

Control rods

Steam outlet to turbine

Uranium breeder blanket

Reactor pool pump

Liquid metal coolant

Steam generator

Water inlet

Heat exchanger transfers heat to steam generator

NUCLEAR POWER FOR TRANSPORTATION

▲ A nuclear-powered icebreaker in the Arctic Ocean

NUCLEAR POWER is also a source of power for some aircraft carriers, submarines, and icebreakers. The advantage of nuclear power over the diesel engines found in most ships is the small amount of fuel required, as nuclear fuel packs in thousands of times more energy than diesel oil.

HOW IT WORKS

A nuclear-powered ship has a small thermal nuclear reactor on board. As in a nuclear power plant, the reactor produces heat, which is used to boil water to make steam.

The steam is fed to a turbine that turns the ship's propeller. The turbine also spins an electric generator that provides electricity for the ship.

NUCLEAR SUBMARINES

The small amount of fuel needed for nuclear reactors is an advantage especially for nuclear submarines. They can carry enough nuclear fuel to stay at sea, hidden underwater, for months on end. The first nuclear-powered submarine was the USS *Nautilus*, launched in 1954. In 1958, it made a famous trip under the Arctic ice cap.

SUBMARINE SINKINGS

Eight nuclear-powered submarines have sunk— two from the United States and six from the ex-Soviet Union and Russia. Their nuclear reactors, all with fuel, and some damaged, remain, trapped in the wrecks. One example is the ex-Soviet K-27. Its reactor overheated in 1968, because of a coolant leak. Nine sailors died from radiation. The vessel was irreparable and was eventually scuttled off northern Russia in 1981.

▲ This Russian-built space probe, *Kosmos,* was powered by a small nuclear reactor.

FACING THE ISSUES

Nuclear-powered ships have to be decommissioned at the end of their lives. Since 1990, Russia has decommissioned nearly 200 nuclear submarines, but dozens are still sitting in dockyards with their nuclear fuel left inside. Some of their reactors and used fuel have been dumped in the Arctic Ocean. Critics of nuclear power are concerned about all these possible sources of dangerous radiation.

NUCLEAR WASTE

FUEL RODS stay in a reactor for about five years, until their energy output begins to decrease. Then they are removed and are known as spent fuel. Spent fuel rods are extremely hot and dangerously radioactive and will stay radioactive for thousands of years. Disposal of this waste is one of the major problems facing the nuclear industry.

STORING WASTE

Spent fuel is moved to cooling ponds on the reactor site, where it stays for decades while it cools down and its radioactivity decreases. Then it is encased in glass and stored in radiation-proof steel or concrete containers. Spent fuel is known as high-level waste because it is so radioactive. Some waste is reprocessed, which means the unused nuclear fuel is removed from the other waste materials and made into new fuel rods.

▲ Under this metal floor is a cooling pond where spent fuel rods are stored.

WHAT DO YOU THINK?

Long-lasting nuclear waste is one of the reasons that antinuclear protesters want to ban nuclear power.

- Are you worried about nuclear waste in the environment?
- Do you trust the nuclear industry to take care of waste properly?
- Is it right to store dangerous waste for future generations to deal with?

THE WASTE PROBLEM

Tens of thousands of tons of high-level nuclear waste are stored around the world. There are 54,000 tons (49,000 t) in the United States alone. At the moment, there are no firm plans for nuclear waste. The most popular plan is to bury it in bunkers hundreds of feet underground until it becomes safe, which will take thousands of years.

TRANSPORTING THE WASTE

Nuclear waste is moved from nuclear power plants to reprocessing plants by train, ship, aircraft, and truck. It is stored in indestructible containers with radioactive shielding. Understandably, the general public is concerned about dangerous waste moving around the countryside, but so far, there have been no major accidents.

▼ Security guards protect a German nuclear-waste train against possible attack by antinuclear protestors.

BUILDING AND DECOMMISSIONING

THE PROCESS OF BUILDING a nuclear power plant begins with the decision to build by a government. There is normally opposition from environmental groups, political parties, and local people, leading to public meetings. The typical lifespan of a reactor is about 30 to 40 years. Then it must be safely taken out of service, or decommissioned.

BUILDING PROJECT

A nuclear power plant is a complex building project. There is not only the reactor to engineer, along with its control and safety features, but also the containment shell, fuel and waste handling equipment and storage, steam generators, turbines, and electric generators. Construction can take 10 years or more, and it involves hundreds of specialty contractors.

◀ A worker prepares the holes through which fuel rods will be inserted during the construction of a new nuclear reactor.

▲ A reactor at Sellafield in the United Kingdom, photographed in 1981, when it was shut down. Decommissioning was still underway in 2008.

DECOMMISSIONING

Decommissioning a nuclear power plant is a difficult and expensive job. The time-consuming and costly part is dismantling the reactor itself because of the radioactive materials inside. Apart from the spent fuel, which is removed and stored, there are other reactor parts that are radioactive because they have been exposed to radiation for decades. Sometimes a reactor is placed under "safe enclosure," when it is left for decades until the radioactivity has died down. Then it can be demolished. Another option is "entombment," when the reactor is covered with a thick layer of concrete that will remain in place for hundreds or thousands of years. Decommissioning a power plant costs one-tenth of the cost of building a new one.

FACING THE ISSUES

It's often stated that nuclear power is "carbon free" because nuclear power plants do not produce carbon dioxide emissions when they are running. However, building and decommissioning a power plant uses energy that comes from fossil fuels and so do mining and processing fuel. Because of this, Greenpeace estimates that the United Kingdoms's planned nuclear power plants will reduce carbon emissions by just 4 percent compared to building efficient coal-fired power plants.

NUCLEAR POWER PLANTS have elaborate safety systems to prevent radioactive materials from escaping into the environment. Despite this, accidents have happened in the past. They range from low-risk leaks from cooling systems to catastrophic meltdowns of reactor cores, such as happened at Chernobyl (See page 28).

▲ A reactor dome at the Kola power plant in Russia. The dome should prevent leakage of radiation in case of an accident.

ACCIDENT CHANCES

Pronuclear enthusiasts argue that the chances of accidents at nuclear power plants are very small and that far fewer people are killed by accidents at nuclear plants than are killed by mining and drilling for oil and coal. Antinuclear protesters argue that there have been many unpublicized near disasters at nuclear power plants, and that a serious accident could affect millions.

REACTOR SAFETY SYSTEMS

If a chain reaction begins to run too fast, or a cooling system fails, there is a danger that a reactor core could overheat and melt. In this case, automatic systems shut down the reactor by fully inserting the control rods. The reactor is also enclosed in a strong concrete shield to stop radiation escaping. The shield also protects the reactor from outside events such as extreme weather.

RUNAWAY REACTOR

In 1979, the core of the Three Mile Island nuclear power plant in Pennsylvania, partially melted down after reaching more than 3,632°F (2,000°C). The cause was the loss of coolant following a stuck valve in the cooling system. The reactor was damaged beyond repair but only a little radiation leaked out.

▼ Three Mile Island nuclear power plant, site of a reactor meltdown in 1979.

FACING THE ISSUES

Studies show that there are no ill effects from living near a nuclear power plant. There was concern when clusters of leukemia (a type of cancer) seemed to occur around nuclear power plants in the United Kingdom and Germany. However, there was never any proof that they were linked to radiation from the power plants.

THE CHERNOBYL DISASTER

THE CHERNOBYL nuclear power plant is close to the city of Prypiat, Ukraine. In 1986, it was the site of the worst nuclear accident of all time. One of the four reactors at the site overheated and exploded, sending radioactive material into the atmosphere. Radiation from the accident caused thousands of deaths.

CAUSES OF THE ACCIDENT

The disaster was caused by a combination of poor reactor design and human error. The reactor began to run out of control, but could not be shut down fast enough as the operators had closed down some of the safety systems. The core overheated and the water coolant turned instantly to steam, leading to a huge explosion that blew open the reactor building. There was no containment shell, and radioactive steam and other debris were released.

THE EFFECTS

Thirty-one workers and firemen died from radiation sickness within three months. A radioactive cloud spread across Europe, reaching as far as the United Kingdom.

▲ The tangled remains of the damaged reactor at Chernobyl, photographed soon after the accident.

Over 333,000 people were evacuated permanently from the area. It is estimated that about 4,000 people who lived close to the plant developed cancer.

CHERNOBYL TODAY

Today, the plant at Chernobyl is covered by concrete, but a new steel shell is planned, as the reactor will be radioactive for thousands of years. Prypiat and Chernobyl are ghost towns. Radiation levels are still dangerously high, and an exclusion zone is still in place. A few people live in the zone, ignoring the risks.

FACING THE ISSUES

When the reactor at Chernobyl exploded, the Soviet authorities tried to stop the news from getting out to the rest of the world. However, they had to own up when high levels of radioactivity were detected in Sweden. The disaster led to safety improvements at other reactors built in the former Soviet Union.

▲ This map shows how radioactive material spread across Europe from the Chernobyl accident.

▼ The deserted and overgrown streets of Chernobyl as they look today.

THERE IS CONCERN that terrorists could ransom a nuclear reactor or cause widespread panic by threatening to release radioactive materials in a populated area. Terrorists could steal nuclear waste and use it to make some sort of bomb or attack a nuclear power plant, allowing radioactive material to escape. The terrorist threat is one reason given by antinuclear protesters for banning nuclear power.

▼ The events of September 11, 2001, alerted the world community to the threat posed by international terrorism.

TRACKING MATERIALS

There are tens of thousands of tons of nuclear waste stored around the world. The nuclear watchdogs or monitoring organizations of countries are responsible for keeping track of their nuclear materials, so that any losses can be reported. Their records can be inspected by the International Atomic Energy Agency (IAEA). There have been attempted thefts from storage bunkers in the countries of the former Soviet Union, where security is often poor.

DIRTY BOMBS

Making a nuclear weapon is extremely difficult, and it is highly unlikely that a terrorist group could ever make one. However, it would be easy to make a so-called "dirty" bomb that used normal explosives to spread radioactive material. The biggest problem facing the authorities would be trying to prevent mass panic if a dirty bomb were detonated in a city.

REACTOR ATTACKS

Governments have understood for a long time that nuclear reactors are potential targets for terrorists. So reactors are well protected by security systems to stop attacks at ground level. However, the 2001 terrorist attacks by passenger planes in the United States made governments ask new questions about the security of nuclear power plants. Some experts suggest that reactor buildings should be strengthened in case of attack from the air. Others think nuclear reactors are hard-to-hit targets, and their concrete containment shells would protect them anyway.

▼ A bomb scare in London. Although a nuclear weapon is beyond the capabilities of terrorist groups, a "dirty" bomb that spreads dangerous radioactive material is a real possibility.

ROGUE STATES

THE FUEL USED in nuclear weapons is produced using some of the same technology that is used in the nuclear power industry. The international community is concerned that some countries are developing nuclear power as a smokescreen for developing nuclear weapons.

▼ U.S. President George W. Bush headed the fight against rogue nuclear states.

WORLDWIDE PROMISES

The Nuclear Non-Proliferation Treaty is an international agreement signed by all the countries in the world except India, Pakistan, Israel, and North Korea. The idea of the agreement is to stop countries from developing nuclear weapons but to allow any country to use nuclear technology peacefully. The IAEA polices the treaty by inspecting nuclear plants around the world.

GET THE FACTS STRAIGHT

- In 2001, following the terrorist attacks of September 11, U.S. President George W. Bush named both North Korea and Iran as members of the "axis of evil" that helped terrorism.

  In 2006, North Korea claimed to have exploded its own nuclear weapon.

▲ After many years of arguments with the international community, North Korean leader Kim Jong-il (center) finally allowed nuclear inspectors into his country.

IRAN

Iran signed the Nuclear Non-Proliferation Treaty, but has regularly broken its promises, leading to a diplomatic battle with the international community. Iran says that it is developing nuclear power plants, but others think it is trying to develop nuclear weapons. In 2003, the IAEA reported that Iran was secretly enriching uranium. The United Nations Security Council ordered Iran to stop enrichment, and put economic sanctions in place. In 2008, the IAEA is still making inspections, and the sanctions are still in place.

NORTH KOREA

North Korea originally signed the Nuclear Non-Proliferation Treaty. In the 1990s, the United States believed that North Korea's only nuclear reactor had produced enough plutonium for a nuclear weapon and threatened air strikes. North Korea withdrew from the Treaty in 2003, after the United States accused it of enriching uranium to make weapons. Late in 2005, North Korea agreed to rejoin the Treaty and to allow IAEA inspectors in. In 2007, it signed an agreement with the U.S. to shut down its reactor in return for energy supplies.

ANTINUCLEAR PROTESTS

▲ Antinuclear protesters outside Sizewell power plant, United Kingdom, in 2007.

SOME ORGANIZATIONS and individuals protest to close down nuclear plants and prevent new ones from being built. Many of their arguments have already been touched on earlier in the book, but here they are in detail, along with some of their key arguments.

ANTINUCLEAR ARGUMENT

The antinuclear movement's list of nuclear problems includes the accidents that allow radiation into the environment, long-term radioactive waste, and the dangers of terrorism and nuclear proliferation. They also argue that nuclear power is hugely expensive, and that it would be better to spend the money on developing renewable and clean-coal technologies. They also point out that nuclear energy is not completely "carbon free," as huge amounts of energy are used to mine, transport, and enrich uranium, as well as to build and decommission the power plants.

PROTESTS AND CAMPAIGNS

Most nuclear protests take the form of nonviolent direct action. Protesters display posters with their messages, hand out leaflets, go on marches, talk to the public, and organize sit-ins that block access to power plants. This all gains them publicity, especially if an event is large enough to be covered by the media.

ANTINUCLEAR SUCCESSES

Public opposition to nuclear power prevented nuclear programs getting off the ground in Ireland and New Zealand. Italy and Ireland held referendums on nuclear power, in which the public voted against it. Existing Italian nuclear power plants were closed down. In Germany, which generates 30 percent of its electricity through nuclear power plants, opposition to nuclear power by political parties led to a decision to phase out nuclear power.

FACING THE ISSUES

Some antinuclear protests have been forceful, with activists taking violent direct action. In 1977, a group known as CARLOS placed explosives at several French nuclear power plants in an attempt to halt the French nuclear power program. And in 2004, a French protester died after being run over by the nuclear waste train he was trying to stop. France continues to use nuclear power and is investing in new power plants.

► This symbol—a red sun on a yellow background—has become the recognized international icon of the antinuclear movement. This German signs says "Nuclear Power? No thank you."

PLANS FOR NUCLEAR POWER

THE NUCLEAR INDUSTRY and pronuclear proponents argue that we need a certain amount of nuclear power to provide a reliable electricity supply. The governments of many countries agree and are planning and building new nuclear power plants. More than 200 new power plants are on the drawing board worldwide.

▼ Early stages in the building of the Flamanville 3 nuclear power plant, France. There has been much protest over the construction of this new-generation nuclear plant.

THE UNITED KINGDOM

In 2008, the UK government gave the go-ahead for new nuclear power plants. The main reasons given were the reduction of both carbon emissions and the reliance on fossil fuels. The reactors will be built and operated by private companies and should be working by 2020. The decision-making process was boycotted by environmentalists, who were convinced that the government had already decided to go ahead. The United Kingdom already faces a bill of around $140 billion to decommission its existing plants.

▲ The opening ceremony for one of China's many new nuclear reactors, designed to help meet the country's expanding energy needs.

THE UNITED STATES

There is renewed interest in nuclear power in the U.S. after a period of 20 years when no new plants have opened. Two-thirds of people who took part in an opinion poll favored more nuclear power. Thirty new plants are planned across the country.

CHINA

China has the most rapidly expanding nuclear program of all, designed to meet the hunger for energy by its growing industries. It plans 88 new plants, using both home-grown and overseas technology, such as the European Pressurized Reactor (See page 40).

FACING THE ISSUES

The Global Nuclear Energy Partnership (GNEP) is a group of countries led by the United States, that plans to organize the reprocessing of spent nuclear fuel. Under its control, the fuel cannot be used to make nuclear weapons.

NUCLEAR FUSION

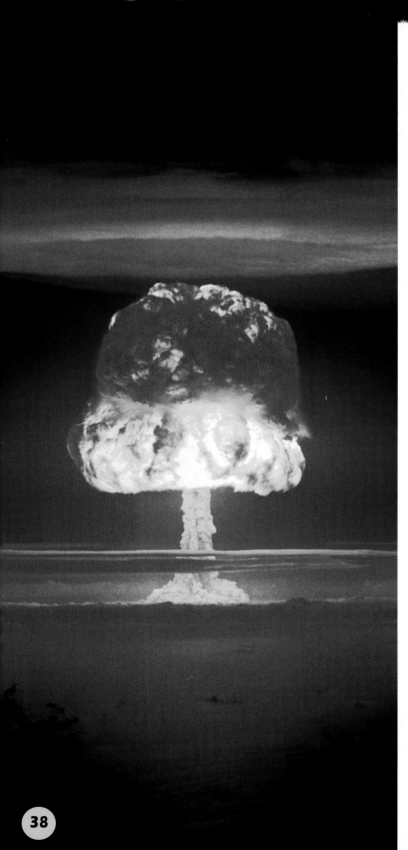

NUCLEAR FUSION is the opposite of fission. During fusion, the nuclei of two atoms join together, releasing energy. Scientists are building experimental fusion reactors, but it could be many decades before we can make electricity this way. If successful fusion reactors could be built, we would have an almost limitless supply of clean energy.

ADVANTAGES OF FUSION

The main advantage of nuclear fusion over nuclear fission is that fusion does not produce large amounts of hazardous radioactive waste. The only product of the reaction is harmless helium gas. Another advantage is that the fuel, a form of hydrogen called deuterium, is extracted from water, so there is a limitless supply. A fusion reactor could never run out of control and cause an explosion.

◄ The awesome power of nuclear fusion is shown in this fusion bomb test. Researchers hope to harness this power for electricity production.

FUSION DIFFICULTIES

To make fusion happen, two nuclei have to smash into each other at a fantastic speed. To make the nuclei move fast enough, the gas in the reactor must be heated to ten times the temperature in the center of the Sun. These temperatures are very hard to create. A second problem is making a container that can both stop the nuclei from escaping and stand up to the immense heat.

FUSION RESEARCH

The largest research reactor to date is the Joint European Torus (JET). It uses a device called a "tokamak" to make a doughnut-shaped magnetic field that contains the super-hot reacting nuclei. Nuclear fusion has happened for a split second in the JET. Work has begun to build the International Thermonuclear Experimental Reactor (ITER) in France, which will be ready to operate around 2020.

GET THE FACTS STRAIGHT

There have been scientific reports of fusion happening at near normal temperatures. This is known as "cold fusion." The first report came from scientists at the University of Utah in 1989. However, there is no proof that cold fusion happens, and most nuclear scientists think it is not possible.

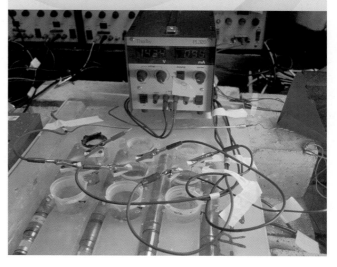

▲ A cold fusion experiment at Oak Ridge National Laboratories in Tennessee. Scientists are divided in opinion as to whether or not cold fusion is possible.

◄ Inside the experimental Joint European Torus (JET) reactor. This is where nuclear fusion may take place one day.

THE NUCLEAR FUTURE

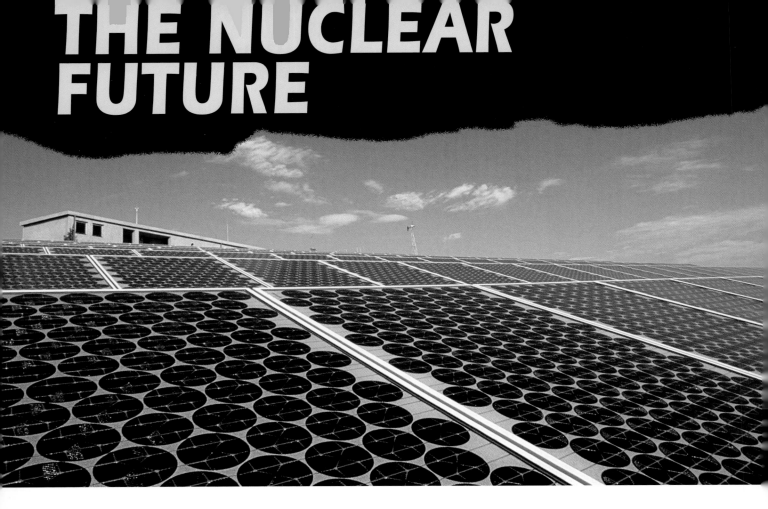

WE WILL ALWAYS NEED sources of energy, and in the future, as the world develops, we'll need more and more. As pressure grows to reduce our use of fossil fuels, and as fossil fuels begin to run out, we will need alternatives. It is likely that nuclear energy will be one of these alternatives, at least in some countries.

▲ It is likely in the future that nuclear energy will be used alongside renewable energy technologies, such as these solar cells.

NEAR-FUTURE REACTORS

The new reactors being built today, such as the European Pressurized Reactor, are known as generation III reactors. Reactors in the research stage that are being designed and tested are known as generation III+ reactors. They should be simpler and cheaper to build and run than current reactors and safer, too. Some of the new designs are "passively safe," which means they can never run out of control.

A FUSION FUTURE

Nuclear fusion, if it could be made to work, promises millions of years of abundant, safe power. However, scientists have not succeeded in producing controlled fusion yet. When the ITER is complete, 20 years of research will follow, and success is not guaranteed. If it does work, there are plans to build a demonstration power plant (DEMO), which would start producing electricity around 2035.

CONCLUSION

Nuclear power has many drawbacks, especially the ongoing problem of what to do with the stockpiles of nuclear waste from today's reactors and the risks of deadly nuclear material leaking from reactors. But if we can overcome these problems, build safer nuclear reactors, and possibly get nuclear fusion working, then nuclear power will be here to stay.

▼ What to do with nuclear waste, such as this, is one of the obstacles facing the promoters of nuclear power.

GET THE FACTS STRAIGHT

If the problems of nuclear power are overcome, in the future we could see nuclear power in many roles other than generating electricity:

● Producing heat for citywide heating systems.

● Producing power to desalinate seawater for coastal cities.

● Producing power to make hydrogen from water, so that hydrogen could be used as a clean fuel.

GLOSSARY

atom One of the extremely tiny particles of which all substances are made.

coal-fired power plant A power plant that burns coal to produce heat to make steam for its turbines.

control rod A rod inserted into a nuclear reactor core to control the speed of the nuclear reactions inside.

coolant A material that carries heat away.

core The central part of a nuclear reactor, where nuclear reactions take place.

decommission Remove from use.

desalinate Remove the salt from seawater, producing fresh water.

enrichment Treating natural uranium to increase the proportion of uranium-235 in it.

fission A nuclear reaction in which the nucleus of an atom splits in two.

fossil fuel A fuel made from the remains of ancient plants and animals. Coal, oil, and gas are fossil fuels.

fuel rod A cylinder of fuel that is inserted into a nuclear reactor core.

fusion A nuclear reaction in which two nuclei join together to form a larger nucleus.

generator A device that produces electricity when its axle is spun round. In a power plant, the axle is spun by a turbine.

greenhouse gas Any gas that traps heat from the Sun in the Earth's atmosphere.

neutron One of the particles that makes up the nucleus of an atom.

nuclear fuel A substance that contains atoms that undergo nuclear reactions, releasing energy.

nuclear reaction When the nucleus of an atom splits in two or two nuclei join together to form a larger nucleus.

nuclear reactor The part of a nuclear power plant where heat is produced to produce steam for the power plant's turbines.

nuclear waste Radioactive material, such as spent (used) nuclear fuel.

nucleus The central part of an atom.

ore Rock that substances are extracted from. For example, uranium is extracted from uranium ore.

proton One of the particles that makes up the nucleus of an atom.

radiation Waves of energy or streams of particles given off by a substance.

radioactive Describes a substance that gives off radiation.

reactor See nuclear reactor.

referendum A public vote held to decide whether a government should carry out a particular policy, such as building nuclear power plants.

scuttle To sink a ship deliberately.

turbine A device with fans that spin at high speed when gas flows through it.

WEB SITES

World Nuclear Association
www.world-nuclear.org
The World Nuclear Association represents the nuclear industry, and promotes the use of nuclear energy for energy production.

Greenpeace
www.greenpeace.org
International site of Greenpeace, the organisation that campaigns against damage to the environment.

International Atomic Energy Agency
www.iaea.org
The International Atomic Energy Agency promotes safe and peaceful use of nuclear energy. It carries out nuclear inspections on behalf of the United Nations.

Global Nuclear Energy Partnership
www.gnep.energy.gov
The Global Nuclear Energy Partnership is made up of countries that want to increase the use of nuclear energy, but without the threat of technology being use for nuclear weapons.

Friends of the Earth
www.foe.org
Website of Friends of the Earth includes discussion of efforts in the United States to build new nuclear power plants.

U.S. Nuclear Regulatory Commission
http://www.nrc.gov/reading-rm/basic-ref/students.html
This page of the U.S. Nuclear Regulatory Commission includes information on nuclear energy, including animations of reactors.

INDEX

accidents 8, 9, 23, 26–29, 34, 41
    Chernobyl 13, 26, 28–29
    Three Mile Island 27
aircraft carriers 12, 20
atoms 8, 10, 11, 14, 15, 17, 18, 38, 42

bombs, "dirty" 30, 31
Bush, George W. 32

China 13, 37

Einstein, Albert 10
emissions, carbon 8, 25, 34, 37

fission, nuclear 10, 11, 14, 15, 18, 38, 42
France 12, 35, 36, 39
fuel, nuclear 8, 9, 11, 14–15, 17, 18, 19, 20, 21, 24, 25, 32, 37, 38, 42
fusion, nuclear 38–39, 41, 42

Germany 11, 13, 23, 27, 35
Greenpeace 25

Hahn, Otto 10

India 13, 32
International Atomic Energy Agency (IAEA) 30, 32, 33
Iran 32, 33
Ireland 13, 35
isotopes 15
Italy 13, 35

Joint European Torus (JET) 39

Meitner, Lise 10
meltdown, nuclear 26–27
moderators 18, 19

neutrons 10, 14, 15, 17, 18, 19, 42
New Zealand 13, 35
North Korea 32, 33
Nuclear Non-Proliferation Treaty 32–33

plants, nuclear power 12, 13, 16–17
    Calder Hall 11
    Flamanville 3 36
    Kola 26
    Sellafield 25
    Sizewell 34
plutonium 11, 14–15, 19, 33
protesters,
    antinuclear 21, 22, 23, 24, 26, 30, 34–35
    pronuclear 26, 36–37

radiation 8, 9, 17, 21, 22–23, 25, 26, 27, 28, 29, 30, 31, 34, 38, 42
reactors,
    advanced gas-cooled 19
    breeder 18, 19
    commissioning 24–25, 33, 34, 36
    decommissioning 13, 21, 24–25, 34, 37, 42
    European Pressurized 37, 40
    International Thermonuclear

    Experimental 39, 41
    pressurized water 18, 19, 37, 40
    thermal 18, 19, 20
rods,
    control 17, 26, 42
    fuel 14–15, 17, 18, 22–23, 24, 42
Russia 13, 21, 26, 28–29, 30

safety, nuclear 26–27
submarines 12, 20–21

terrorism 8, 30–31, 32, 33, 34

United Kingdom (UK) 11, 12, 25, 27, 28, 31, 34, 37
United States (U.S.) 11, 12, 21, 23, 27, 30, 31, 32, 33, 37, 39
uranium 9, 14–15, 19, 33, 34, 42

waste, nuclear 8, 9, 22–23, 24, 25, 30, 34, 35, 37, 38, 41, 42
weapons, nuclear 8, 11, 30, 31, 32–33, 37

Here are the lists of contents for each title in *Science in the News*:

CLIMATE CHANGE

WHAT IS CLIMATE CHANGE? • CLIMATE-CHANGE SCIENCE • CLIMATE-SCIENCE HISTORY
CLIMATE CHANGE IN THE PAST • CAUSES OF CLIMATE CHANGE • CARBON DIOXIDE EMISSIONS
THE EFFECTS OF CLIMATE CHANGE • CLIMATE-CHANGE REPORTS • PIONEER INTEREST GROUPS
CLIMATE-CHANGE SUMMITS • GOVERNMENT REACTIONS • NEW INDUSTRIAL NATIONS
CONTINUING PROTESTS • AGAINST THE FLOW • CARBON REDUCTION • PREDICTING THE FUTURE
RESPONDING TO CLIMATE CHANGE

ORGAN TRANSPLANTS

INTRODUCTION • IN THE BEGINNING • WORLD FIRSTS • ORGAN CRISIS • PRESUMED CONSENT
LIFE FROM LIFE • RELIGION & CULTURE • ARTIFICIAL ORGANS • XENOTRANSPLANTATION
STEM CELL RESEARCH • THE RIGHT TO AN ORGAN? • TRANSPLANT TOURISTS • ORGAN SELLERS
REGULATING THE TRADE • POSTOPERATIVE LIFE • FACE TRANSPLANTS • NEW BREAKTHROUGHS

COSMETIC SURGERY

INTRODUCTION • ANCIENT ORIGINS • WORLD WAR I AND WORLD WAR II
FROM HOLLYWOOD TO MAIN STREET • SURGICAL TREATMENTS • NONSURGICAL TREATMENTS
THE BENEFITS • THE RISKS • SURGERY ADDICTS • TEENAGE SURGERY • CHECKS AND BALANCES
THE SURGEONS • VIEWING FIGURES • "THE BEAUTY MYTH" • BOOM AND BUST
ALTERNATIVES • FACING THE FUTURE

NUCLEAR POWER

WHAT IS NUCLEAR POWER? • THE HISTORY OF NUCLEAR POWER
WHO USES NUCLEAR POWER? • NUCLEAR FUELS • NUCLEAR POWER PLANTS • NUCLEAR REACTORS
NUCLEAR POWER FOR TRANSPORTATION • NUCLEAR WASTE • BUILDING AND DECOMMISSIONING
NUCLEAR SAFETY • THE CHERNOBYL DISASTER • TERROR THREATS • ROGUE STATES
ANTINUCLEAR PROTESTS • PLANS FOR NUCLEAR POWER
NUCLEAR FUSION • THE NUCLEAR FUTURE

GENETICS

SHINING MICE AND SUPER CROPS • HISTORY 1: BLASPHEMY! • HISTORY 2: PARENTS AND OFFSPRING
USING INHERITANCE—FOR BETTER AND WORSE • ANIMAL ODDITIES, PECULIAR PLANTS • A CODE FOR LIVING
THE CHANGING CODE • UNLUCKY INHERITANCE • FRANKENSTEIN FOODS? • DANGEROUS MEDDLING?
MAKING MONSTERS? • "FINGERPRINTS" • ARE YOU MY PARENTS? • NATURE AND NUTURE
ALTERED INHERITANCE • A CARBON COPIES

MAKING A NEW LIFE

INTRODUCTION • HISTORY 1: MAGIC AND MYSTERY • HISTORY 2: SOLVING THE PROBLEM
THE GIFT OF LIFE: 1 • PARENT PROBLEMS • EXTRA EGGS AND EXTRA HELP • SAFETY IN NUMBERS?
THE GIFT OF LIFE: 2 • TWO MOTHERS? • TOO OLD FOR PARENTHOOD? • CHECKING PROGRESS
BOYS OR GIRLS? • SAVIOR SIBLINGS • FUTURE PROOF • WHAT IS A CLONE?
HUMAN CLONES • THE FUTURE